SAS/ASSIST® Software: Your Interface to the SAS® System

Version 6
First Edition

SAS Institute Inc.
SAS Circle □ Box 8000
Cary, NC 27512-8000

The correct bibliographic citation for this manual is as follows: SAS Institute Inc., *SAS/ASSIST® Software: Your Interface to the SAS® System, Version 6, First Edition,* Cary, NC: SAS Institute Inc., 1990. 64 pp.

SAS/ASSIST® Software: Your Interface to the SAS® System, Version 6, First Edition

Copyright © 1990 by SAS Institute Inc., Cary, NC, USA.

ISBN 1-55544-375-3

All rights reserved. Printed in the United States of America. No part of this publication may be reproduced, stored in a retrieval system, or transmitted, in any form or by any means, electronic, mechanical, photocopying, or otherwise, without the prior written permission of the publisher, SAS Institute Inc.

1st printing, May 1990

The SAS® System is an integrated system of software providing complete control over data access, management, analysis, and presentation. Base SAS software is the foundation of the SAS System. Products within the SAS System include SAS/ACCESS,® SAS/AF,® SAS/ASSIST,® SAS/CPE,® SAS/DMI,® SAS/ETS,® SAS/FSP,® SAS/GRAPH,® SAS/IML,® SAS/IMS-DL/I,® SAS/OR,® SAS/QC,® SAS/REPLAY-CICS,® SAS/SHARE,® SAS/STAT,® SAS/CONNECT,™ SAS/DB2,™ and SAS/SQL-DS™ software. Other SAS Institute products are SYSTEM 2000® Data Management Software, with basic SYSTEM 2000, CREATE,™ Multi-User,™ QueX,™ Screen Writer,™ and CICS interface software; NeoVisuals® software; JMP™ and JMP IN™ software; SAS/RTERM® software; and the SAS/C® Compiler. *SAS Communications,® SAS Training,® SAS Views,®* and the SASware Ballot® are published by SAS Institute Inc. Plink86® and Plib86® are registered trademarks of Phoenix Technologies Ltd. All other trademarks above are registered trademarks or trademarks, as indicated by their mark, of SAS Institute Inc.

A footnote must accompany the first use of each Institute registered trademark or trademark and must state that the referenced trademark is used to identify products or services of SAS Institute Inc.

The Institute is a private company devoted to the support and further development of its software and related services.

SAS/ASSIST Software . . . Your Window to the SAS System

SAS/ASSIST software opens up to you the full scope and power of the SAS System. Its menus let you focus on your task quickly and easily. You've got online help at every point and clear instructions on every screen. And, the view's pretty exciting!

Why is SAS/ASSIST software exciting? Well, it depends on who you are.

If you're a new SAS user
- You don't need to learn a new language. You just "point and click."
- You have an online tutorial to get you going.

If you're an occasional SAS user
- You don't have to remember anything about the SAS System, except what it can do for you. You don't have to recall the SAS language or any rules of syntax. SAS/ASSIST software guides you through every task.

If you're an experienced SAS user
- You can prototype and test applications quickly.
- You can save the code that SAS/ASSIST software generates for you and modify it later. Or you can add it to larger applications.

If you work in the Information Center
- All your SAS users will have the same interface with the SAS System, regardless of the operating system or hardware they're using.
- You can develop a menu front end for your existing SAS applications.
- You can develop new applications that have the look and feel of SAS/ASSIST software.

But No Matter Who You Are . . .

☐ Once you learn SAS/ASSIST software under one system, you know it for all systems.

Yes, there are a couple of differences from system to system, but they're minor. Your method of interacting with SAS/ASSIST software may differ, depending on whether you have a mouse, and your filenames may differ, depending on the conventions of your operating system. That's about it.*

☐ No matter whether you're on a mainframe, a mini, or a workstation, SAS/ASSIST software comes out to meet you like a PC program does. It's clear, and it's friendly.

☐ You can pull in your data from an external source or enter them through SAS/ASSIST software.

☐ You can get to the SAS System more easily than ever before to

☐ **access** your data
☐ **manage** your data
☐ **analyze** your data
☐ **present** your data.

☐ Your life is about to get a whole lot easier.

Your Window to SAS/ASSIST Software

This manual introduces you to SAS/ASSIST software. The first sections of this book show you the software's features; the latter sections of the book show you how to get your own work started on the software.

When you are ready to try SAS/ASSIST software at your terminal, find out how to log on and off, how to invoke the SAS System, and how to identify your terminal and hardcopy graphics device. Use the inside front cover to jot down that information for future reference.

---

* This book demonstrates SAS/ASSIST software under MVS, using IBM Corporation's Model 2 3279 terminal.

And When You Open the Window . . .

You get the same view, whether your computer is sitting next to you ...

... or far away in the computer room.

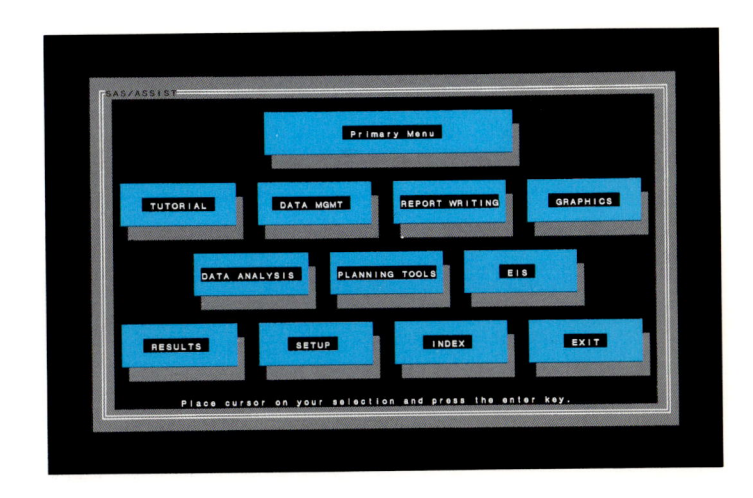

You can start your task right away. You have everything you need.

Now then—enjoy!

Contents

1 . . . . **Introducing SAS/ASSIST Software**
Shows you how to produce a report and a graph with SAS/ASSIST software.

15 . . . . **The SAS System at Your Fingertips**
Describes each choice on the Primary Menu and shows sample results from each choice.

33 . . . . **What You Need to Run SAS/ASSIST Software**
Lists the software and hardware needed to run SAS/ASSIST software.

35 . . . . **Getting Started with SAS/ASSIST Software**
Shows how to invoke SAS/ASSIST software and create your own SAS data set.

47 . . . . **SAS/ASSIST Software — Your Window to Greater Productivity**
Gives you a last look at SAS/ASSIST software and a quick look at the whole SAS System.

49 . . . . **Index**

Credits

Documentation

Composition..............Mary Cole

Graphic Design..........Creative Services Department

Proofreading.............Gwendolyn Colvin, Toni Sherrill

Technical Review.......Stuart Austin, Pat Berryman,
Deva Kumar,
Kathy Roggenkamp

Writing and Editing....Miguel Bamberger, Rick Cornell,
Sally Craig

Software

SAS/ASSIST software has been implemented by the Applications Development Department (led by Kathy Roggenkamp) of the Display Products Division (led by Deva Kumar). Contributions and support were given to the project by members of the Applications Division, Core Division, Graphics Division, and Host Systems Division.

Development
John Crouch, Tom Dickey, Gul Ege, Sandy Emerson, Tammy Gagliano, Peter Herbertz, Gail Kramer, Deva Kumar, John Larus, Kathy Roggenkamp, Sharon Sanders, Cliff Schell

Developmental Testing
Su Cleveland, Mini Gupta, Angela Huggins, Carol Thompson, Linda Wharton, Melissa Williams

Quality Assurance Testing
Jacqueline Allen, Stuart Austin, Brendan Bailey, Pat Berryman, Debbie Johnson, Kari Richardson

Technical Support
Ann Carpenter, Jim Goodling, Annette Harris, Yvonne Selby

Introducing SAS/ASSIST® Software

SAS/ASSIST software is a task-oriented, menu-driven interface that gives you "point and click" access to the SAS System.

SAS/ASSIST software is for everyone who needs to

- ☐ write reports
- ☐ manage data
- ☐ analyze data
- ☐ produce presentation graphics
- ☐ produce QC charts
- ☐ make business forecasts
- ☐ manage projects
- ☐ develop applications.

You can make selections with your mouse or with your terminal's TAB and ENTER keys. Either way, SAS/ASSIST software brings you the power of the SAS System without your having to write code.

This section shows you how SAS/ASSIST software produces a report and a chart. Later, after you read "Getting Started with SAS/ASSIST Software" (page 35), you can come back here and reproduce these tasks on your terminal. For the time being, just relax and observe the process on paper.

Here's the Primary Menu for SAS/ASSIST software.

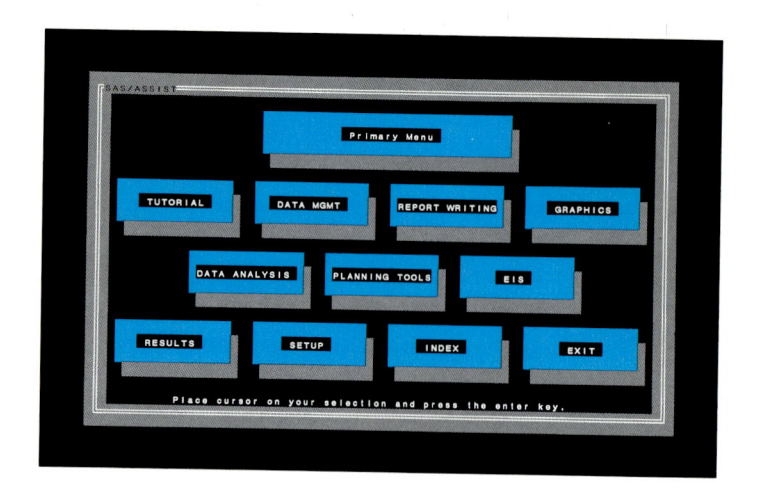

And here's a report that was produced with just a few steps.

Write Reports Quickly

To create the report shown on the previous page, start by selecting **REPORT WRITING** from the Primary Menu. The Report Writing Menu appears.

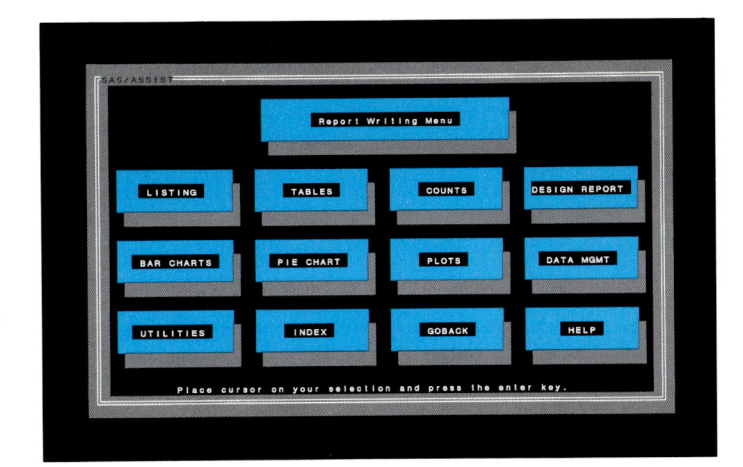

Help is always available.

INDEX gives you direct access to all report writing tasks.

The Report Writing Menu offers you several report styles. Select **LISTING**.

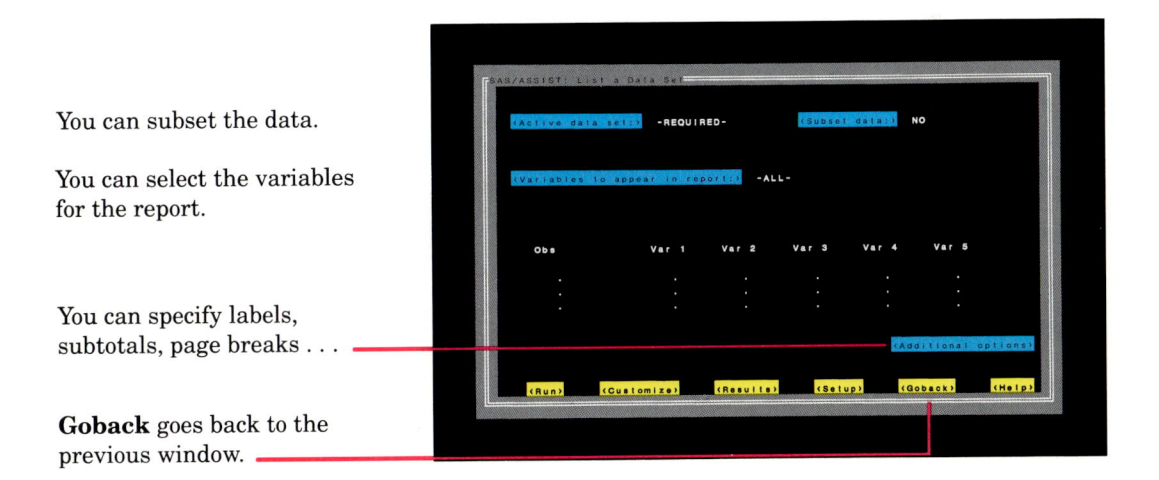

You can subset the data.

You can select the variables for the report.

You can specify labels, subtotals, page breaks . . .

Goback goes back to the previous window.

Select your data by placing the cursor in the **Active data set** field and pressing ENTER.

4   Introducing SAS/ASSIST Software

A list of the SAS data sets known to your session appears.

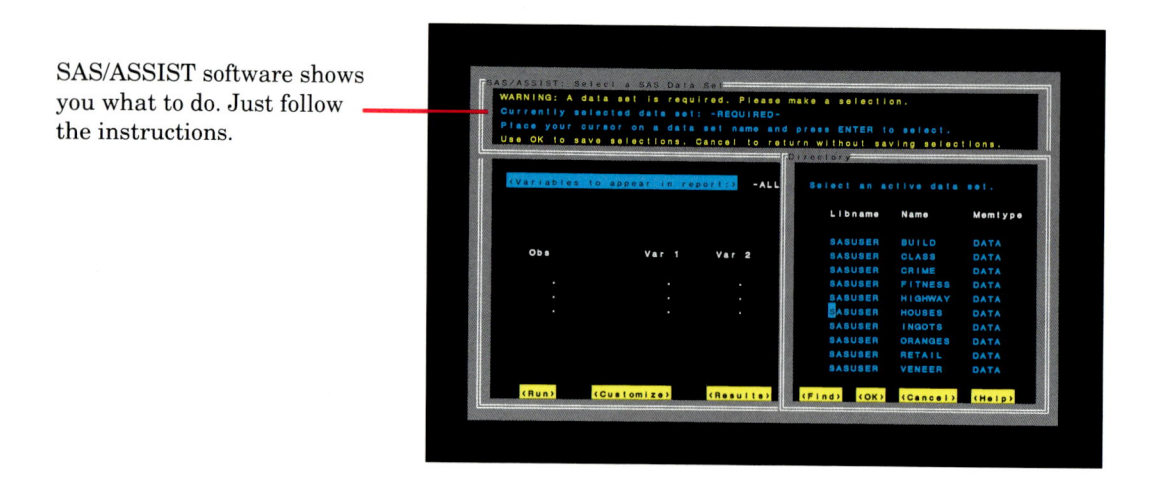

SAS/ASSIST software shows you what to do. Just follow the instructions.

Select the HOUSES data set.

Then, to exclude some variables from the report, select **Variables to appear in report**.

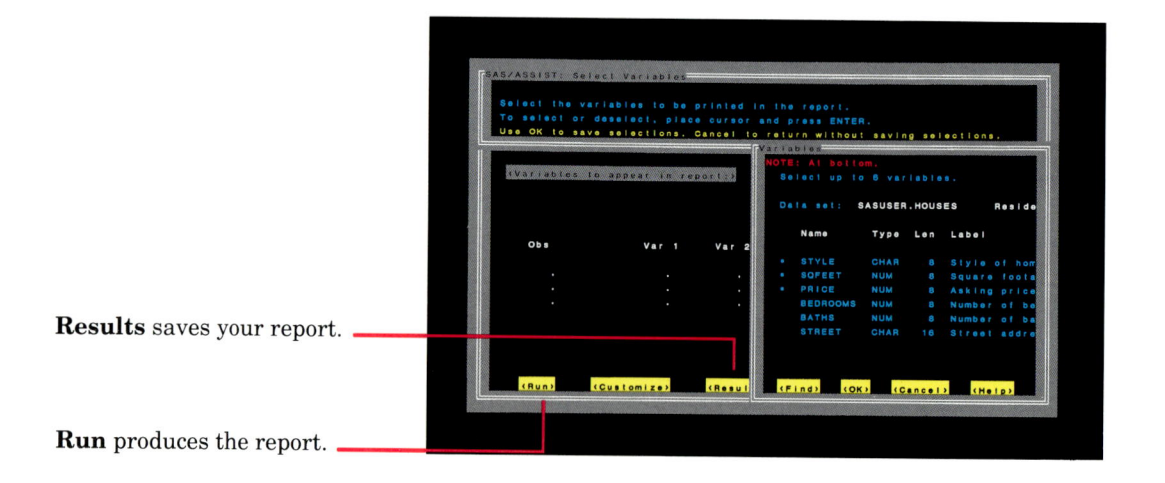

Results saves your report.

Run produces the report.

Select the variables you want printed; they will appear in the order you select them. Save your choices by selecting **OK**. Select **Run** to produce the report.

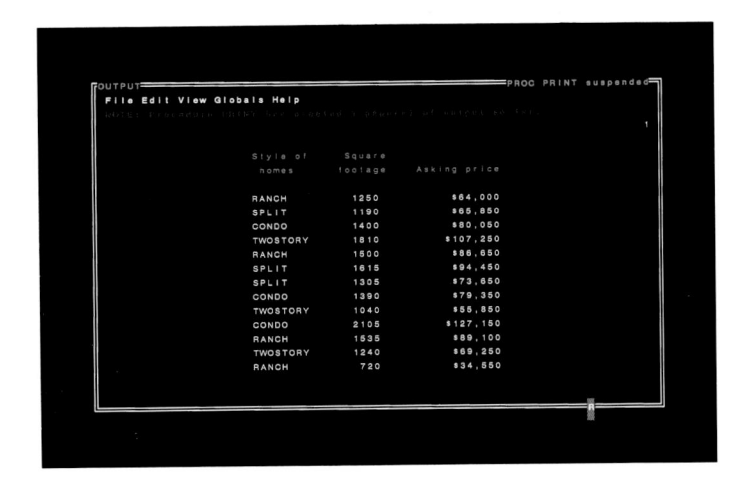

![Screenshot of OUTPUT window showing a PROC PRINT report with columns: Style of homes, Square footage, Asking price]

```
┌OUTPUT═══════════════════════════════════════════PROC PRINT suspended┐
│ File Edit View Globals Help                                          │
│                                                                    1 │
│                                                                      │
│                    Style of      Square                              │
│                    homes         footage    Asking price             │
│                                                                      │
│                    RANCH         1250       $64,000                  │
│                    SPLIT         1190       $65,850                  │
│                    CONDO         1400       $80,050                  │
│                    TWOSTORY      1810       $107,250                 │
│                    RANCH         1500       $86,650                  │
│                    SPLIT         1615       $94,450                  │
│                    SPLIT         1305       $73,650                  │
│                    CONDO         1390       $79,350                  │
│                    TWOSTORY      1040       $55,850                  │
│                    CONDO         2105       $127,150                 │
│                    RANCH         1535       $89,100                  │
│                    TWOSTORY      1240       $69,250                  │
│                    RANCH          720       $34,550                  │
│                                                                      │
└──────────────────────────────────────────────────────────────────────┘
```

To exit the report, select **File**. When the File pull-down menu appears, select **End**.

Note: To close a pull-down menu without making a selection, move the cursor out of the window. You may also need to press ENTER or click the mouse.

If the pull-down menu shows Exit instead of End, select **ASSIST** from the Globals pull-down menu to return to your window.

6 Introducing SAS/ASSIST Software

Customize Output

Suppose you want the report to have a title.

First, select **Customize**.

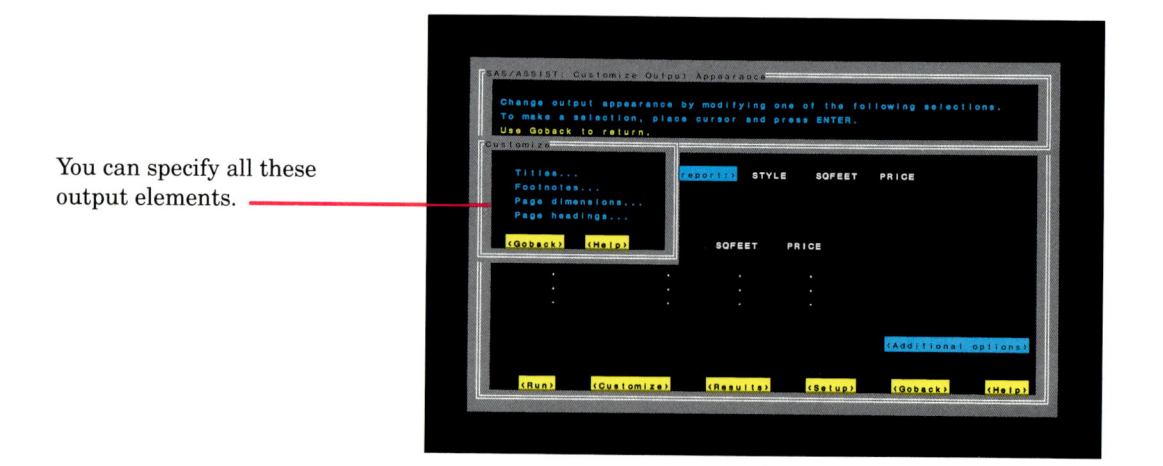

You can specify all these output elements.

Select **Titles** as the output element to be customized.

Introducing SAS/ASSIST Software 7

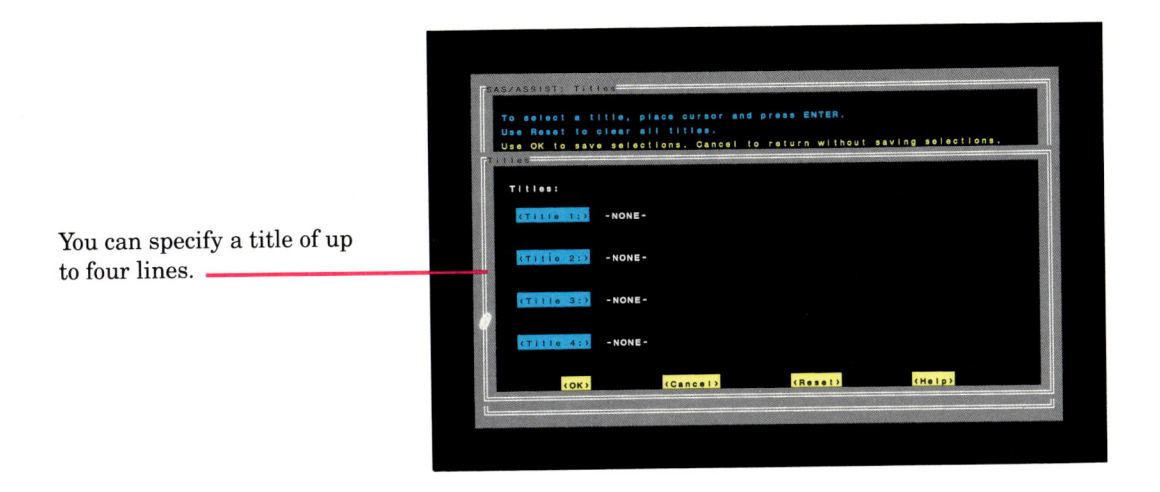

You can specify a title of up to four lines.

Select **Title 1**. When the Title 1 window appears, type the first line of your title.

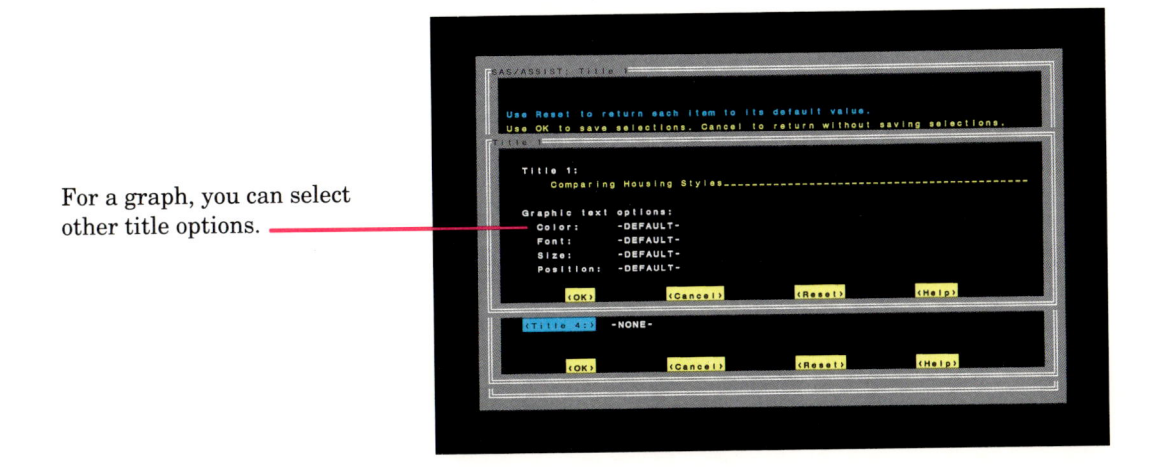

For a graph, you can select other title options.

After saving your title selections, select **Run** to produce the report. It should look like the one on page 2. After you view the report, select **Goback** to return to the Primary Menu.

8 Introducing SAS/ASSIST Software

Produce Presentation Graphics Quickly

Suppose you want to graph your data.* Here's a bar chart of the housing data presented earlier.

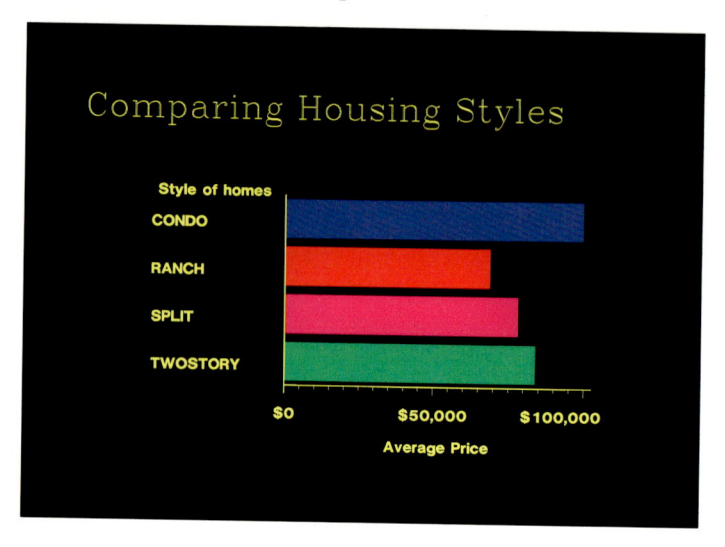

[Bar chart titled "Comparing Housing Styles" showing Style of homes: CONDO, RANCH, SPLIT, TWOSTORY plotted against Average Price from $0 to $100,000]

The next few pages show the selections that created the bar chart.

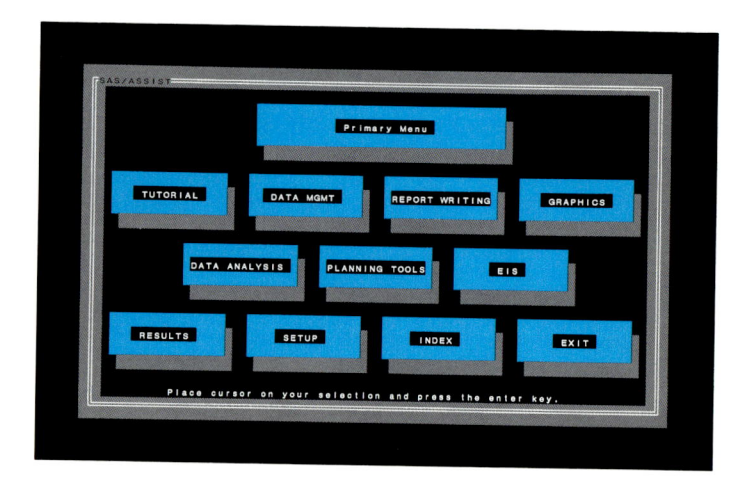

[SAS/ASSIST Primary Menu screen showing buttons: TUTORIAL, DATA MGMT, REPORT WRITING, GRAPHICS, DATA ANALYSIS, PLANNING TOOLS, EIS, RESULTS, SETUP, INDEX, EXIT. Instruction: "Place cursor on your selection and press the enter key."]

To start, select **GRAPHICS**.

---

* You need a graphics terminal to do this.

Introducing SAS/ASSIST Software   9

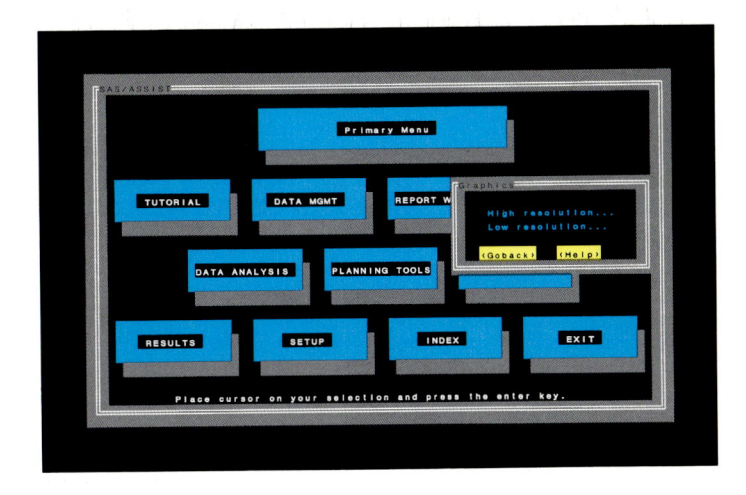

Now select **High resolution**.

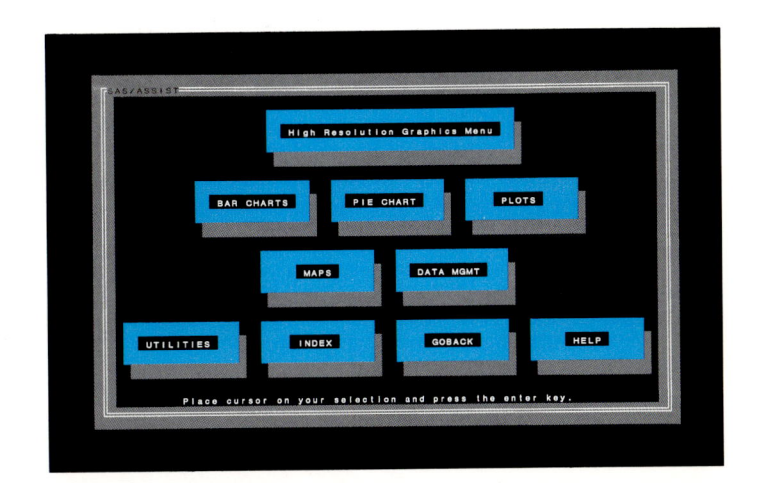

INDEX gives direct access to graphics tasks.

UTILITIES replays and creates data for graphics.

Select **BAR CHARTS**. When the Bar Charts window appears, select **Horizontal bar charts**.

10 Introducing SAS/ASSIST Software

You can easily choose which chart style you want.

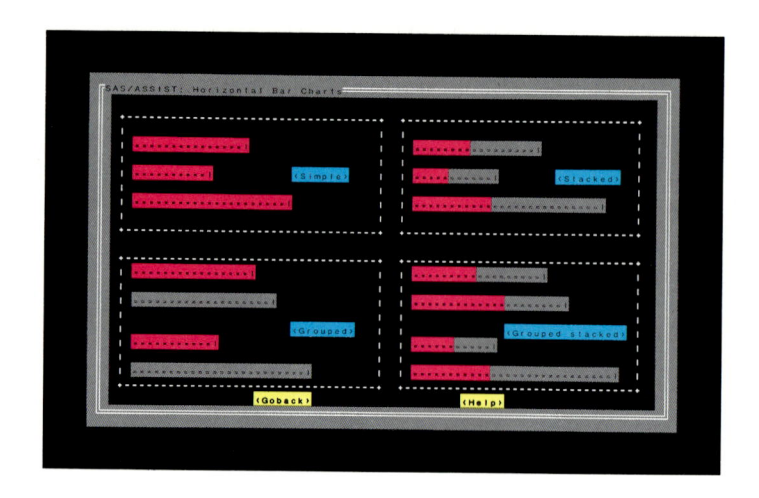

Select **Simple**.

(When you try out this chart, be sure you know the name of your graphics terminal before continuing because you'll need it in a minute.)

Your active data set is saved from task to task and from session to session.

You can select the variable to be charted along the vertical axis.

You can also specify the statistic to be displayed for bar values.

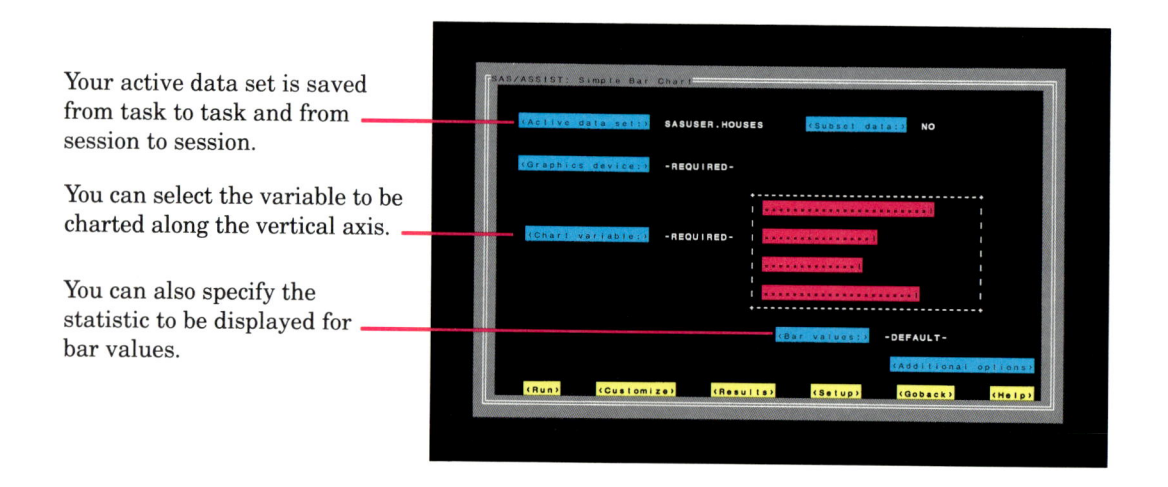

Select **Graphics device**. When the Active Graphics Device window appears, select **Display device**. A list of supported devices appears.

Select your graphics device. You can scroll the list to find the device. Or since the list is quite long, you can select **Find** to shorten the search.

The "radio buttons" in the Find dialog box simplify all your SAS/ASSIST tasks.

You can
- select search order
- specify context
- specify case sensitivity.

Simply point and click!

Type in the terminal name and select **OK**. When the device name appears, select it.

Return to the Simple Bar Chart window and select **Chart variable** to specify the variable to be charted along the vertical axis.

12 Introducing SAS/ASSIST Software

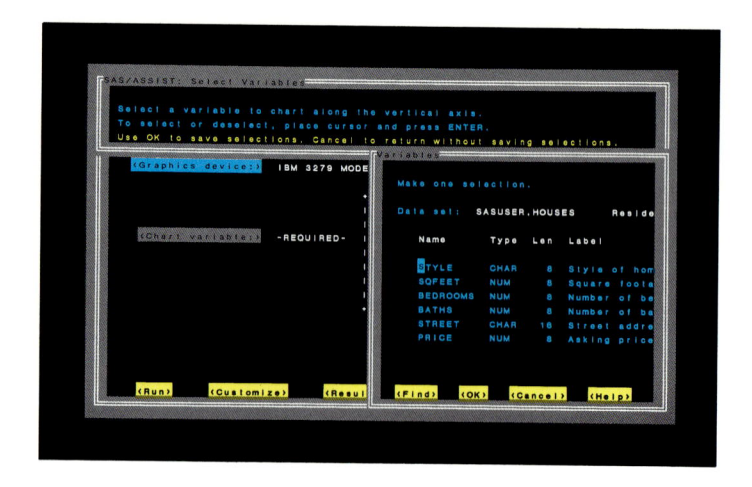

When the variable list appears, select **STYLE**.

Say you want to show the average price for each style. Select **Bar values** to specify this statistic.

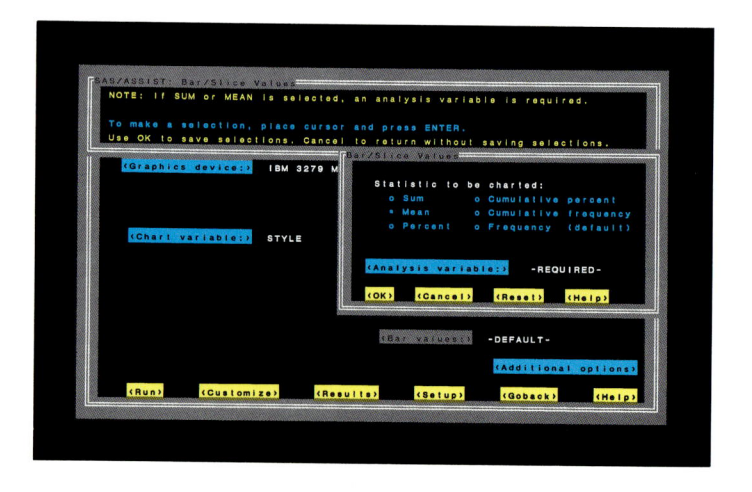

When the Bar/Slice Values window appears, select **Mean** and then select **Analysis variable** to choose the variable you want to summarize.

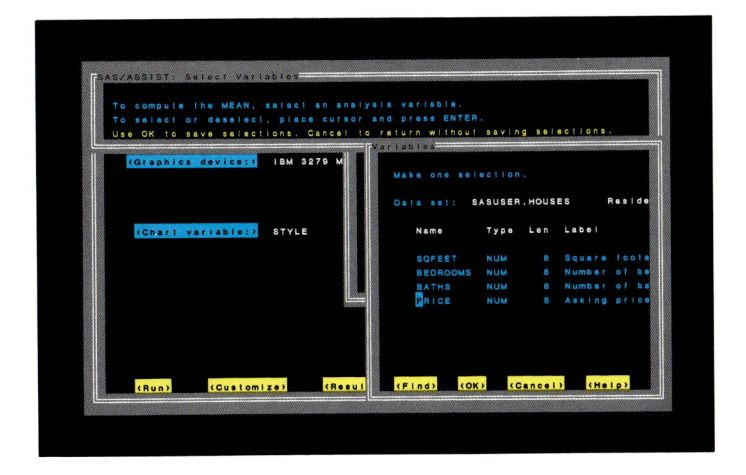

From the list of variables, select **PRICE.** After saving your selections, select **Additional options** to change the label for the horizontal axis. Then, as each window comes up, select **Axis options**, **Horizontal axis**, and **Axis label**.

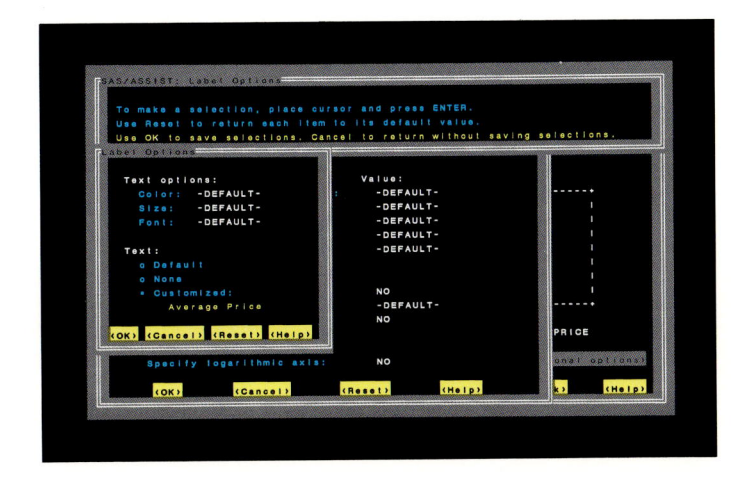

In the Label Options window, select **Customized** and type *Average Price*.

Save your selections and produce the chart again. As before, you can select **Customize** to specify a new title.

Looking Ahead

Now you've seen SAS/ASSIST software prepare a report and a chart.

Next, you'll see examples of output from many more tasks, such as data management, data analysis, project management, statistical quality control, and business forecasting.

The SAS® System at Your Fingertips

SAS/ASSIST software gives you easy access to base SAS software and other components of the SAS System.

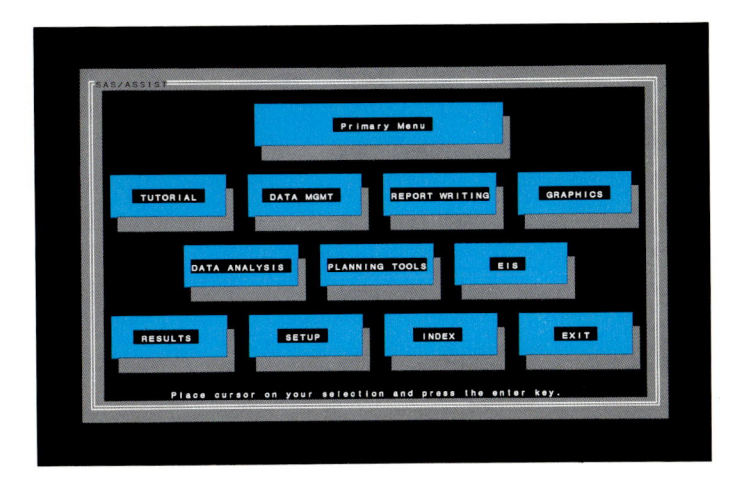

The next few pages show menus or windows that exemplify each of the options on the Primary Menu. Where appropriate, sample results are also shown.

Tutorial

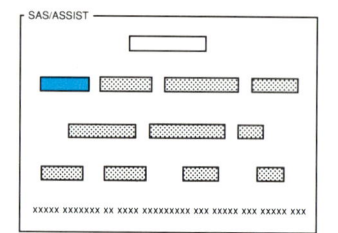

The TUTORIAL option provides an orientation to both SAS/ASSIST software and the SAS System.

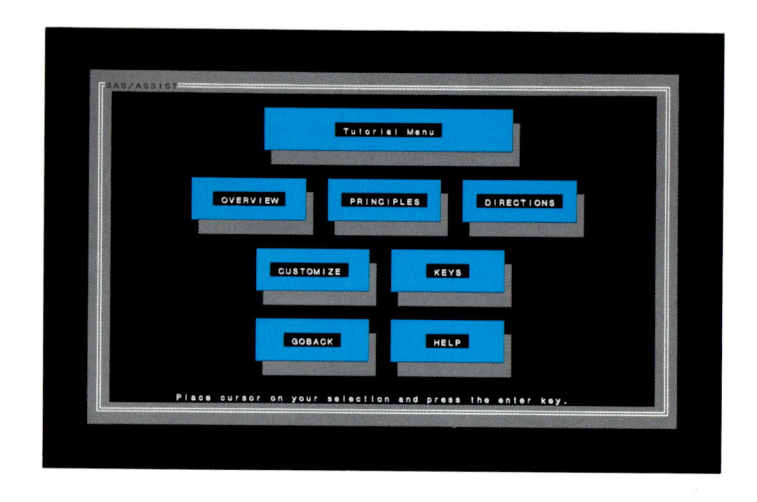

Principles of working with the SAS System.

Directions for using SAS/ASSIST software.

Customizing SAS/ASSIST software.

Setting function keys.

When you select **DIRECTIONS** on the Tutorial Menu, you find instructions on how to use the various windows. For example, the window below illustrates how to make selections when you list a SAS data set.

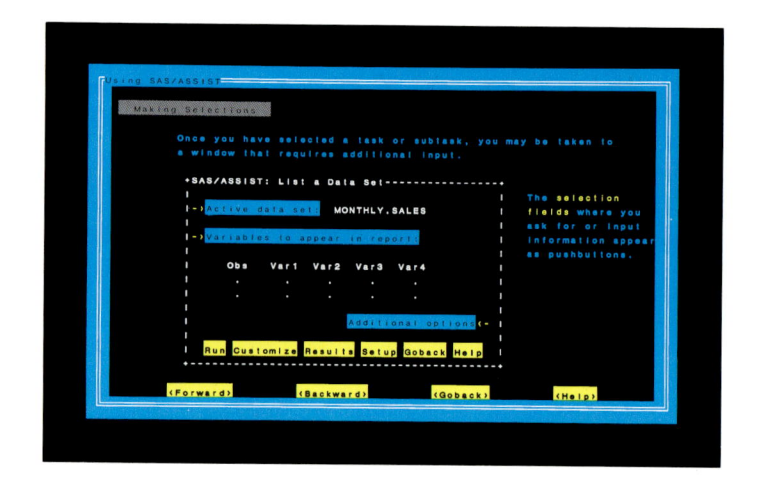

The SAS System at Your Fingertips **17**

Data Management

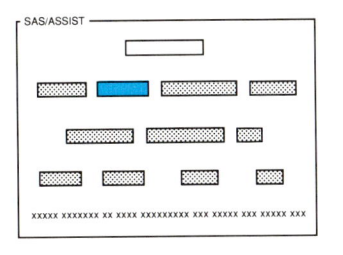

SAS/ASSIST software lets you do a wide variety of data management tasks.

You can edit or browse SAS data sets.

You can create SAS data sets by
- entering data interactively
- importing data from flat files.

You have direct access to data from databases and other types of files.

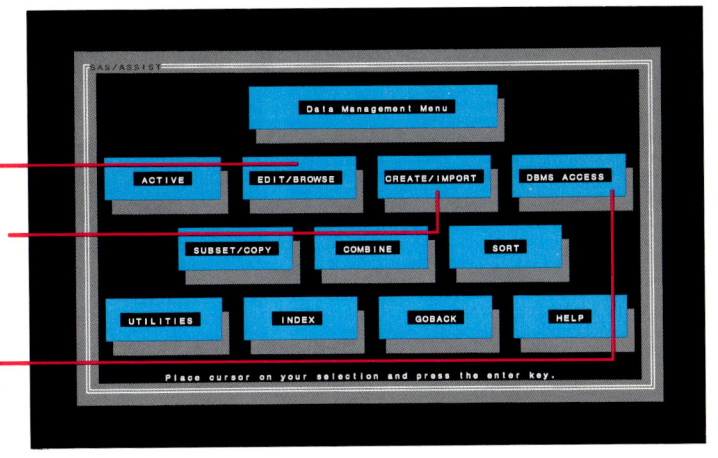

When you create SAS data sets for certain tasks, the software prompts you for the data. For example, suppose you need to create a data set for data to be shown on a map of Europe. First, the software gives you a list of available maps.

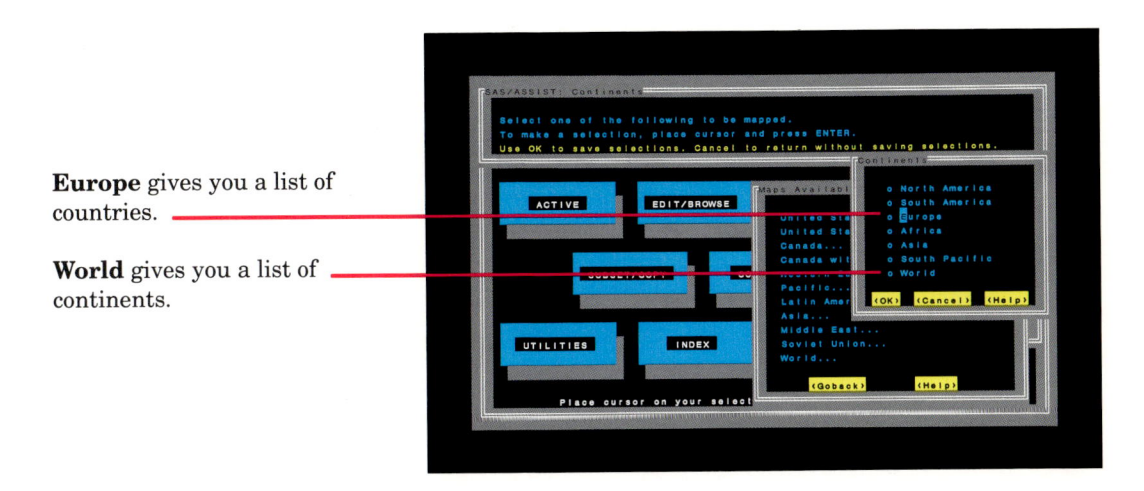

Europe gives you a list of countries.

World gives you a list of continents.

Then, you can enter the data for each country.

You can sort a data set, create one data set from another, or combine two data sets into one. You can specify which observations or variables you want in the new data set.

Your choices are easy to pick!

You can also

☐ transport a data library to or from a different system
☐ convert a Version 5 data library to Version 6 format
☐ view the contents of a data set, create formats, and so on.

Report Writing

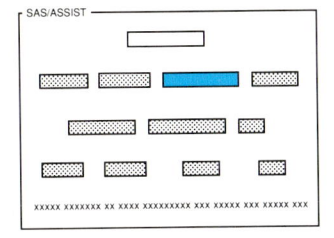

You have already seen how easy it is to produce a simple report with SAS/ASSIST software. You can also produce other kinds of reports.

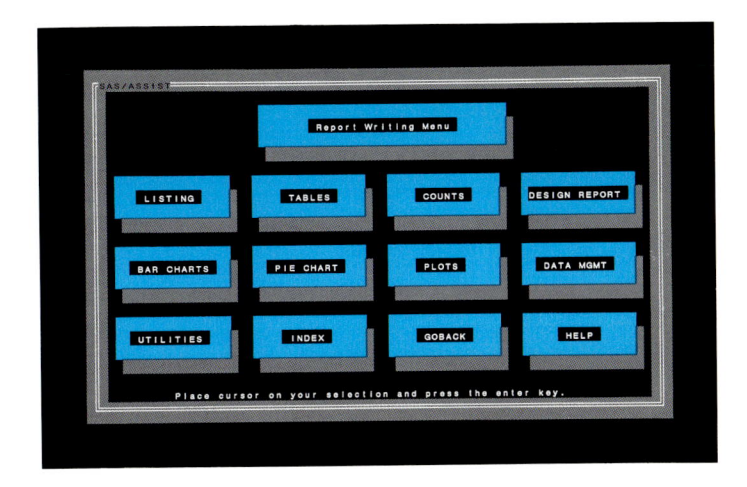

For example, selecting **TABLES** opens the following window, from which you can choose the style for your report.

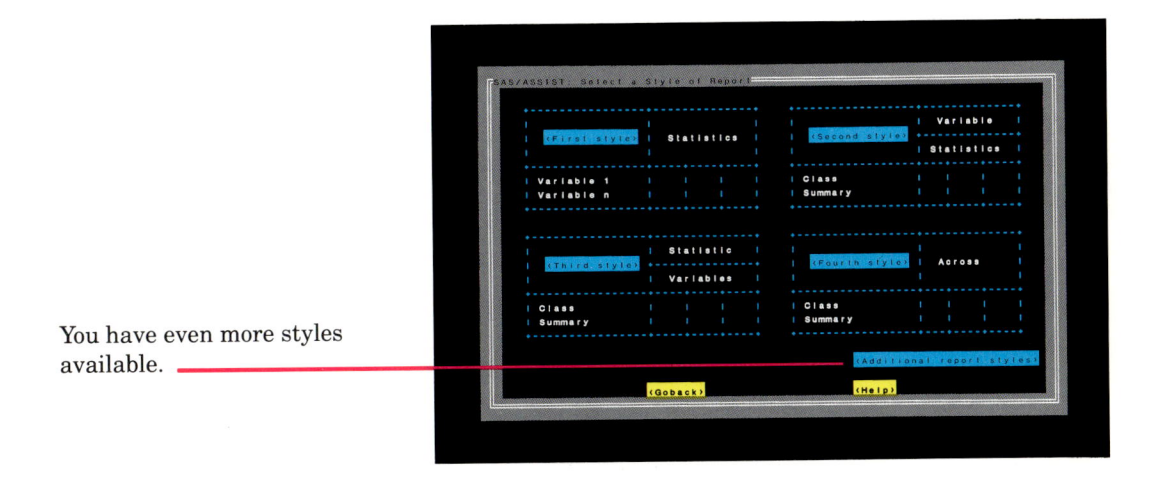

You have even more styles available.

As shown earlier in this book, it takes just a few steps to produce a report like this:

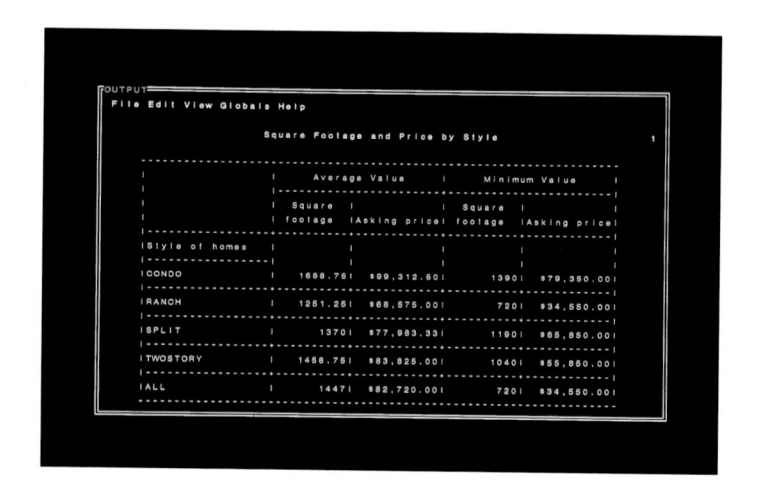

```
OUTPUT
File  Edit  View  Globals  Help

                    Square Footage and Price by Style                      1
  ---------------------------------------------------------------------
  |                  |    Average Value    |    Minimum Value     |
  |                  |---------------------+----------------------|
  |                  |  Square  |          |  Square  |           |
  |                  |  footage |Asking price| footage |Asking price|
  |------------------|----------+----------+----------+-----------|
  |Style of homes    |          |          |          |           |
  |------------------|          |          |          |           |
  |CONDO             |  1688.75 | $99,312.50|   1390  | $79,350.00|
  |------------------|          |          |          |           |
  |RANCH             |  1251.25 | $68,575.00|    720  | $34,550.00|
  |------------------|          |          |          |           |
  |SPLIT             |  1370    | $77,983.33|   1190  | $65,850.00|
  |------------------|          |          |          |           |
  |TWOSTORY          |  1488.75 | $83,825.00|   1040  | $55,850.00|
  |------------------|          |          |          |           |
  |ALL               |  1447    | $82,720.00|    720  | $34,550.00|
  ---------------------------------------------------------------------
```

Besides producing simple reports and tables, you can

- create tables of frequencies of values in a data set
- create or modify a report interactively
- produce line printer vertical and horizontal bar charts
- produce line printer pie charts
- produce line printer plots of one variable against another
- create labels and calendars
- create data sets for specific tasks.

Graphics

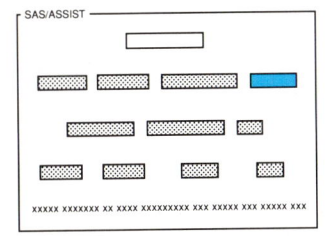

You have already seen how SAS/ASSIST software can be used to produce bar charts. You can also use it to

- ☐ produce pie charts
- ☐ produce plots of one variable against another
- ☐ produce maps at various scales for most regions of the world
- ☐ replay graphs
- ☐ produce test patterns for the current device driver
- ☐ create data sets for particular types of graphics.

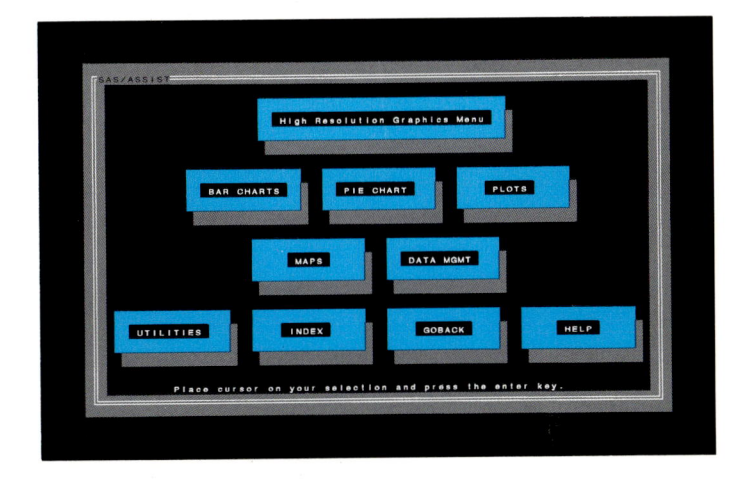

For example, to produce a map of Europe, you would start by selecting **MAPS**.

Then you would select the variable whose values are to be displayed on the map. The variable is in a SAS data set that contains map information. Pages 17 and 18 show you how to create such a data set.

The resulting map might look like the one shown below.

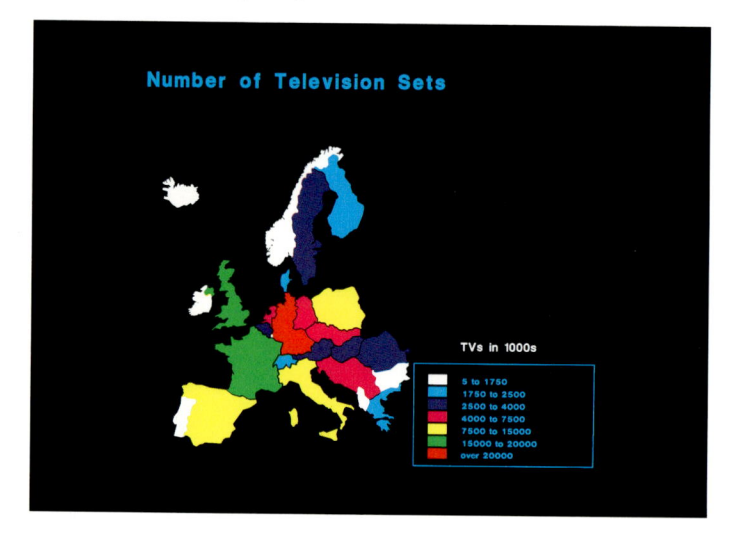

Data Analysis

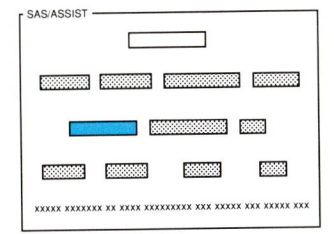

SAS/ASSIST software offers several analysis tools. You can

- produce frequency tables or compute summary statistics, correlations, or confidence intervals about the mean
- perform linear regression, logistic regression, or regression with correction for autocorrelation
- perform analysis of variance, nonparametric ANOVA, or *t*-tests
- compute principal components or canonical correlations
- perform seasonal adjustment of time series
- compute percentiles, standardize or rank data, create time series data, and convert frequency of time series data.

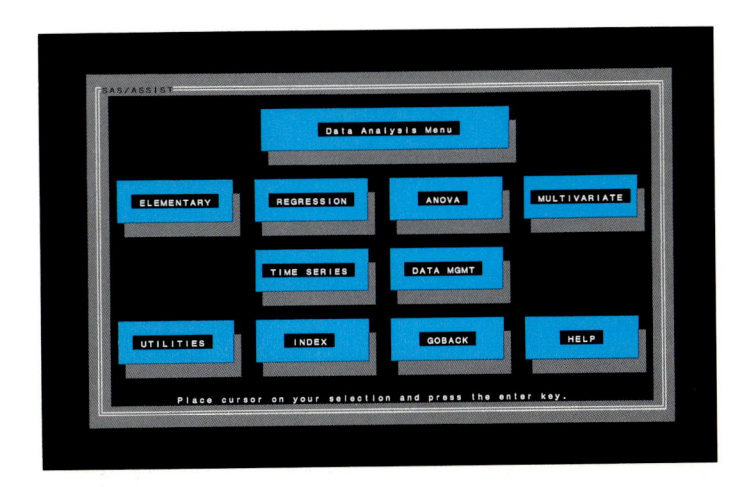

For example, a regression analysis is simple to perform. The output shown next was obtained from data in the FITNESS data set. It shows a regression analysis for oxygen consumption and running time data, as well as a plot of the data.

24 The SAS System at Your Fingertips

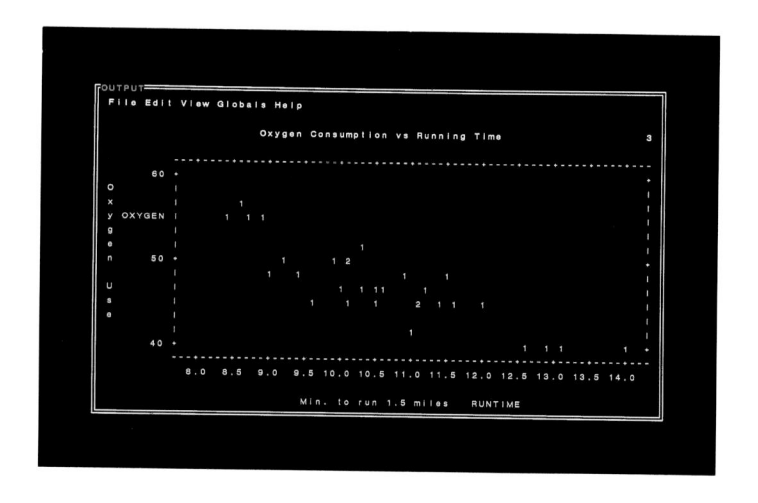

```
┌OUTPUT═══════════════════════════════════════════════════PROC REG suspended═┐
│ File Edit View Globals Help                                                │
│                                                                            │
│                         Sum of        Mean                                 │
│        Source    DF    Squares       Square     F Value    Prob>F          │
│                                                                            │
│        Model      1   426.30515    426.30515    79.710     0.0001          │
│        Error     29   155.09823      5.34821                               │
│        C Total   30   581.40338                                            │
│                                                                            │
│          Root MSE      2.31262    R-square    0.7332                       │
│          Dep Mean     47.33177    Adj R-sq    0.7240                       │
│          C.V.          4.88598                                             │
│                                                                            │
└────────────────────────────────────────────────────────────────────────────┘
```

```
┌OUTPUT══════════════════════════════════════════════════════════════════════┐
│ File Edit View Globals Help                                                │
│                     Oxygen Consumption vs Running Time               3     │
│                                                                            │
│            60 +---------------------------------------------------+        │
│        O      |                                                   |        │
│        x      |             1                                     |        │
│        y OXYGEN |         1  1 1                                  |        │
│        g      |                                                   |        │
│        e      |                           1                       |        │
│        n   50 +                     1  2                          |        │
│               |              1  1              1   1              |        │
│        U      |                     1  1 1 1                      |        │
│        s      |                      1  1    2  1 1 1             |        │
│        e      |                              1                    |        │
│            40 +--------------------------------------1--1-----1---+        │
│                8.0  8.5  9.0  9.5 10.0 10.5 11.0 11.5 12.0 12.5 13.0 13.5 14.0 │
│                              Min. to run 1.5 miles    RUNTIME              │
└────────────────────────────────────────────────────────────────────────────┘
```

Planning Tools

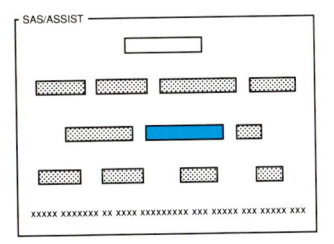

SAS/ASSIST software includes planning tools. You can

- analyze and compare loans
- design and analyze experiments
- produce control charts and perform capability analysis
- perform project management tasks
- forecast time series.

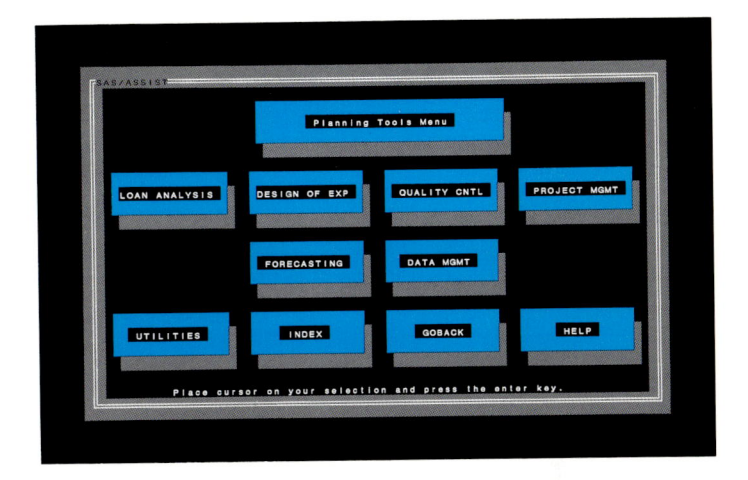

For example, you can generate a GANTT chart.

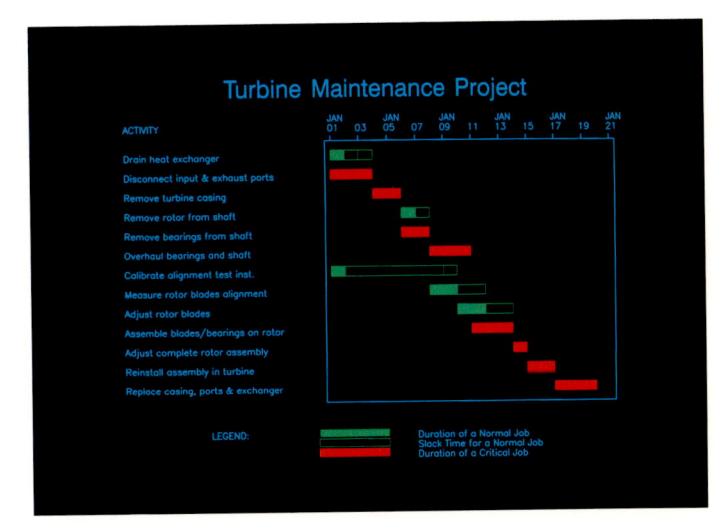

26 The SAS System at Your Fingertips

Or, you can produce a control chart.

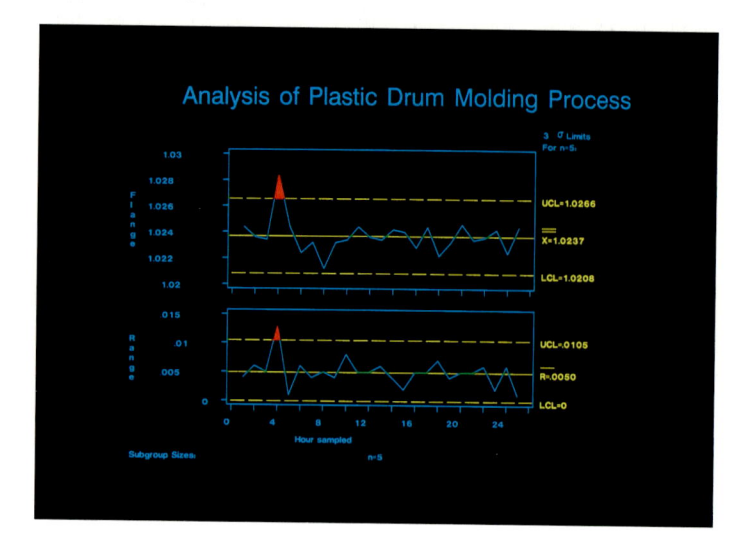

Executive Information System

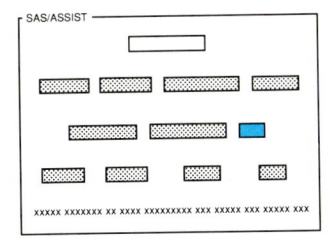

With SAS/ASSIST software, you can easily create and access your own applications, in effect extending the tasks that can be performed with the product.

You can build menu-driven applications that include
- graphs
- reports
- executable programs
- host commands
- desktop applications.

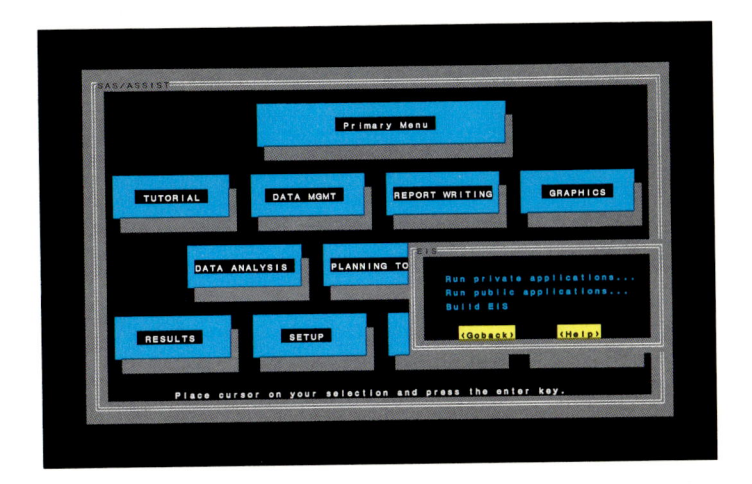

You can also access desktop applications developed by SAS Institute by selecting **Run public applications** and **Desktop Applications**.

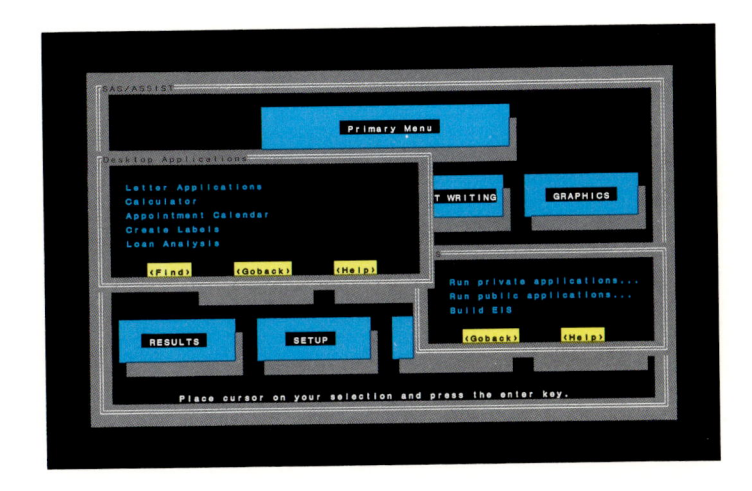

Results

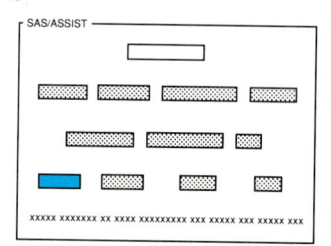

Most SAS/ASSIST options create SAS programs to perform your tasks. You can save any of these programs, or their output, by selecting **Results** from the task window, then access them later with the RESULTS option on the Primary Menu. This option enables you to

- recall a program or output
- edit a program
- execute a program
- redisplay a graph
- delete a program or output from the catalog
- rename a program or output.

For example, assume you had saved the program used for regression analysis shown earlier. You would access that program now by first selecting **Access saved programs**.

[screen image showing SAS/ASSIST: Access Saved Programs directory with OXYVSRUN SOURCE entry]

Then you could select the program, modify it for a different task, and execute it again. The program appears as shown below. As you can see, it's fully documented, so you can change it easily.

[screen image showing the SAS program listing]

```
00001  /*------------------------------------------------------*
00002   | Summary:                                              |
00003   |     This program uses PROC REG to generate a regression analysis. |
00004   |     Current data set:SASUSER.FITNESS                  |
00005   | Generated: 13MAR90  9:47:38                           |
00006   *------------------------------------------------------*
00007   | The OPTIONS statement specifies the dimensions of the printed |
00008   | output in characters per line and lines per page and whether or |
00009   | not the current date and page number are printed.     |
00010   *------------------------------------------------------*
00011
00012  options linesize=76 pagesize=27 nodate number pageno=1;
00013  /*------------------------------------------------------*
00014   | TITLE statements specify text printed at the top of the output |
00015   | page.                                                 |
00016   *------------------------------------------------------*
00017  title1 'Oxygen Consumption vs Running Time';
00018  proc reg data=SASUSER.FITNESS;
00019       model OXYGEN = RUNTIME ;
00020       plot (OXYGEN)*(RUNTIME) ;
```

Setup

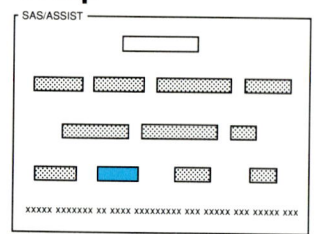

The SETUP option on the Primary Menu lets you control certain aspects of the SAS session in which you are working. Among other things, you can

- associate reference names with any data libraries or files you need to use
- manage device drivers and printing forms
- sort data sets
- review your current function keys.

The Setup option is also available within most SAS/ASSIST tasks.

Index

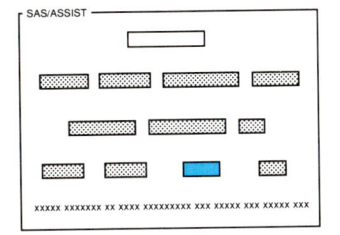

The INDEX option provides an alphabetic selection list of all tasks that can be performed with SAS/ASSIST software. If you do not see the task you want to do listed on a menu, look for it in the primary index. Selecting an item from the Index window takes you to the task.

Exit

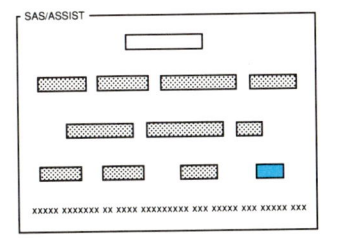

When you select the EXIT option, you leave SAS/ASSIST software.

General Features

In addition to all the task-specific features available with each option, SAS/ASSIST software includes several features that are available across all options.

- You can enhance your output. For example, you can add text for titles and footnotes for most applications, as well as control the page size.
- As previously mentioned, programs can be stored. In addition, you can preview the program through a special preview window.
- A UTILITIES option available from many menus lists additional tasks available in that area.
- An INDEX option available from each menu provides an alphabetic selection list of all tasks available in that area.
- You can limit a task to selected observations or specified groupings of observations.
- Help is available from every window. Also, you can press the HELP key while in any field for information on that field.
- You can enter a question mark (?) in any data entry field for a selection list or more information.

What You Need to Run SAS/ASSIST® Software

To run SAS/ASSIST software you need

- ☐ a userid on a computer system that runs the SAS System
- ☐ a terminal that supports full-screen displays.

SAS Software Requirements

The following SAS software must be licensed and installed on the computer system:

- ☐ base SAS software, Release 6.06
- ☐ SAS/ASSIST software, Release 6.06.

Certain tasks require other products for full functionality. These tasks and the products they require are listed here:

Task	Software Required
data management	SAS/FSP
data analysis	SAS/STAT
high-resolution graphics	SAS/GRAPH
DBMS access	SAS/ACCESS
EIS	SAS/AF*
quality control	SAS/QC
forecasting	SAS/ETS
design of experiments	SAS/QC
project management	SAS/OR
time series	SAS/ETS

* SAS/AF software is needed to invoke the AF application.

Getting Started with SAS/ASSIST® Software

This chapter shows how to invoke SAS/ASSIST software and use it to create your own SAS data set.

Invoking SAS/ASSIST Software

Before you can invoke SAS/ASSIST software, you must log on and call the SAS System.

(Depending on your operating system, you can invoke the SAS System to use either the SAS Display Manager System or a native windowing interface.)

How you invoke SAS/ASSIST software depends on whether you have an action bar in the PROGRAM EDITOR window when the display manager screen appears.

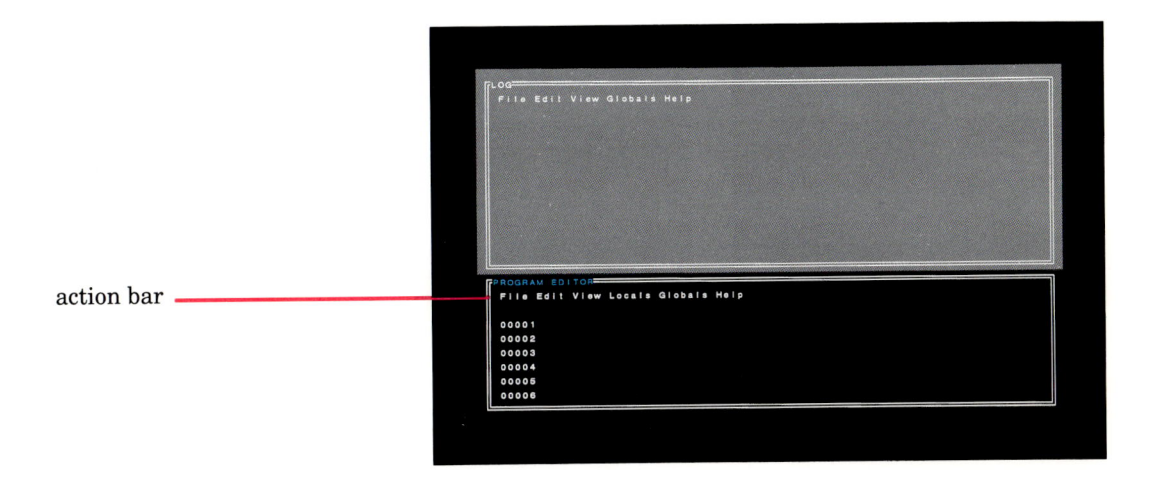

action bar

If you have an action bar, select **Globals**. That is, move your cursor to **Globals** and press the ENTER key. (Or use a mouse.)

36 Getting Started with SAS/ASSIST Software

[screenshot of LOG and PROGRAM EDITOR windows with Globals pull-down menu showing: ASSIST, Program Editor, Log, Output, Output Manager, Graph Manager, Invoke SAS/AF application..., Data management, Desktop, Command, Global options]

When the Globals pull-down menu* appears, select **ASSIST**.

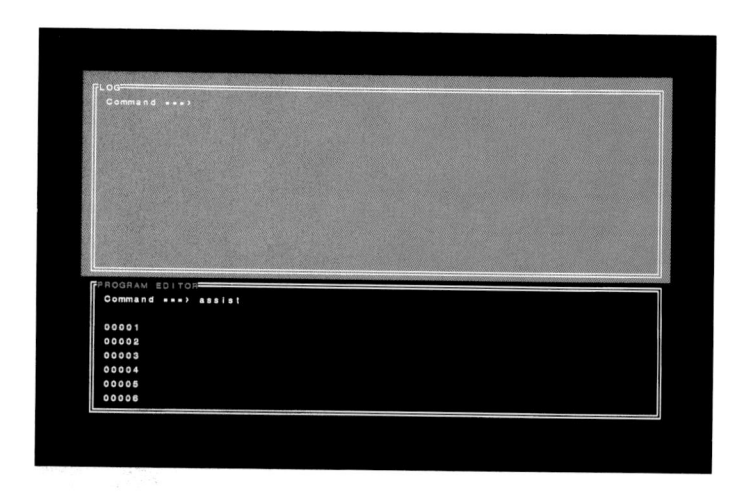

[screenshot of LOG and PROGRAM EDITOR windows with "assist" typed on the command line]

If you do not have an action bar, as shown above, simply type *assist* on the command line.

(If you are already familiar with the SAS Display Manager System, note that its function key definitions extend to SAS/ASSIST software.)

---

* To close a pull-down menu without making a selection, move the cursor out of the window. You may also need to press ENTER or click the mouse.

You see the Primary Menu for SAS/ASSIST software. If this is the first time you invoke the software, the Primary Menu appears after the sample data sets are created.

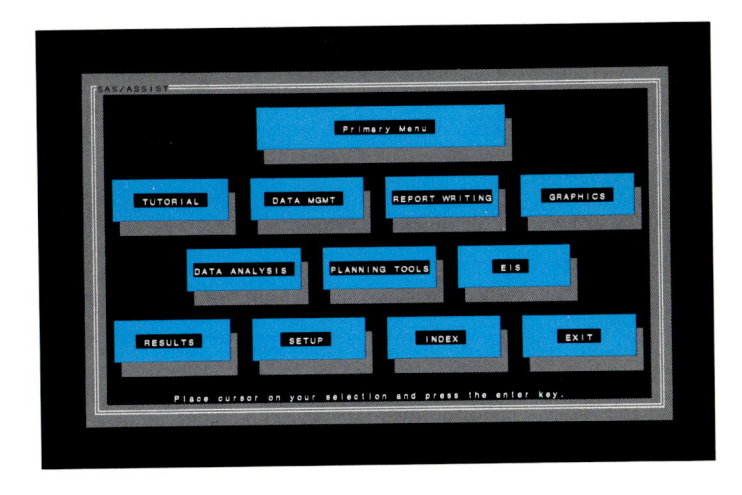

This window, as well as others within SAS/ASSIST software, may look different from the one on your display, depending on your terminal characteristics.

Getting Acquainted

Now that you have invoked SAS/ASSIST software, try out a couple of things. You might want to start by selecting **TUTORIAL**, to become familiar with the software.

Then go back to the beginning of this book and follow the report writing demonstration on your terminal.

Creating Your Own SAS Data Library

To use SAS/ASSIST software with your data, you may want to have your data in SAS data sets, which, in turn, must reside in a data library.

To create your data library, follow the instructions on the next few pages.

Select **SETUP** from the Primary Menu.

Then select **SAS data libraries**.

When the SAS Data Libraries window appears, select **Assign a new libref**. A *libref* is the name you assign to a SAS data library during a session. It forms the first part of a permanent SAS data set name.

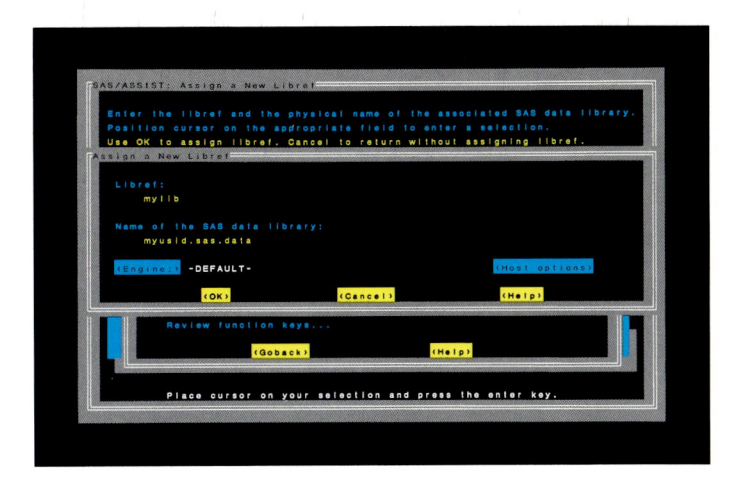

```
┌─ SAS/ASSIST: Assign a New Libref ──────────────────────────────┐
│  Enter the libref and the physical name of the associated SAS data library. │
│  Position cursor on the appropriate field to enter a selection.             │
│  Use OK to assign libref. Cancel to return without assigning libref.        │
│ ┌─ Assign a New Libref ─────────────────────────────────────┐ │
│ │   Libref:                                                 │ │
│ │       mylib                                               │ │
│ │                                                           │ │
│ │   Name of the SAS data library:                           │ │
│ │       myusid.sas.data                                     │ │
│ │                                                           │ │
│ │   (Engine)  -DEFAULT-                         (Host options) │
│ │              (OK)         (Cancel)              (Help)    │ │
│ │                                                           │ │
│ │   Review function keys...                                 │ │
│ │              (Goback)              (Help)                 │ │
│ └───────────────────────────────────────────────────────────┘ │
│        Place cursor on your selection and press the enter key. │
└────────────────────────────────────────────────────────────────┘
```

1. Enter the libref you want to use. (This example uses MYLIB.)
2. Enter the name of the physical file in which you want to store the data.

   ☐ Under MVS, enter a fully qualified OS data set name (for example, MYUSID.SAS.DATA). If the data set is not allocated, the software prompts you for the required information.

   ☐ Under CMS, enter the filemode (for example, A).

   ☐ Under other operating systems, enter the name of a directory or subdirectory. For example, under VMS, you would enter [MYDIR].

3. Select **OK**.

SAS/ASSIST software responds with a message indicating that the libref was successfully assigned.

Now you have a library in which to store your data sets. The next section tells you how to create a data set.

40 Getting Started with SAS/ASSIST Software

Creating Your Own Data Set

How you create a SAS data set depends on whether you are importing data that reside in an external file or entering data interactively.

As an example for discussing both methods, assume you want to process the following data:

JAN	3051.23	JUL	4711.44
FEB	2813.50	AUG	4627.56
MAR	3214.87	SEP	4001.47
APR	3471.09	OCT	3365.98
MAY	3943.78	NOV	2978.12
JUN	4561.52	DEC	3123.19

Importing Data

If your data are already in a file, follow these steps to create a SAS data set:

1. From the Primary Menu, select **DATA MGMT**.
2. From the Data Management Menu, select **CREATE/IMPORT**.
3. From the Create/Import Menu, select **Import data from flat file**.
4. From the Import Data from Flat File window, select **Data file to import**.
5. Enter the name of the file containing the data and select **OK**. The following table shows sample filenames under various operating systems.

Operating System	**Sample Filename**
AOS/VS	:UDD:mydir:sales.dat
CMS	sales.data
MVS	myusid.sales.data
OS/2®	A:sales.dat
PRIMOS®	<MFD>mydir>sales.dat
UNIX®	/usr/myusid/sales_dat
VMS™	[mydir]sales.dat

OS/2 is a registered trademark of International Business Machines Corporation.
PRIMOS is a registered trademark of Prime Computer, Inc.
UNIX is a registered trademark of AT&T.
VMS is a trademark of Digital Equipment Corp.

Getting Started with SAS/ASSIST Software **41**

6. From the Import Data from Flat File window, select **Output data set**. The following window is displayed:

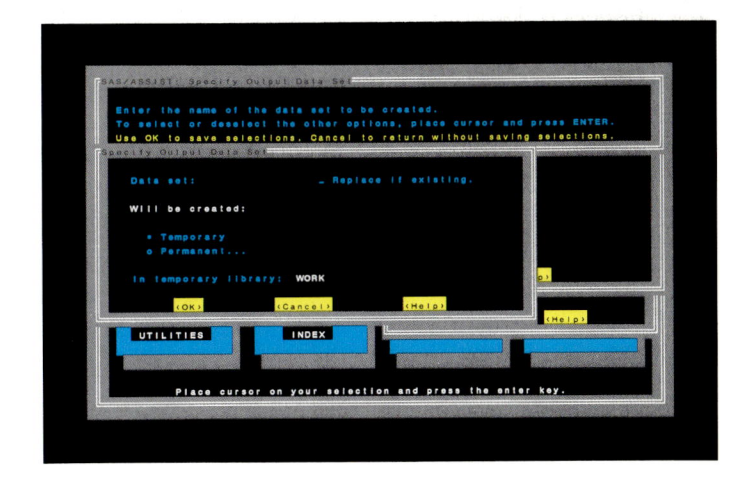

a. Enter the name of the SAS data set (for example, REVENUE).
b. Select **Permanent**. The software displays a list of your available SAS data libraries. Select the data library you just created (see page 39).
c. Select **OK.**

Under MVS, the Import Data from Flat File window should resemble the one shown next.

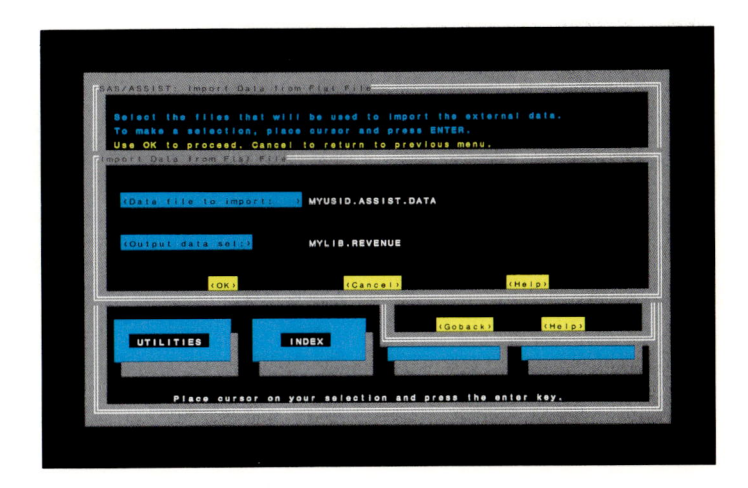

42 Getting Started with SAS/ASSIST Software

7. In the Import Data from Flat File window, select **OK**.
8. In the Define Fields window, use angle brackets to mark the fields. Select **OK** when all the fields are marked.

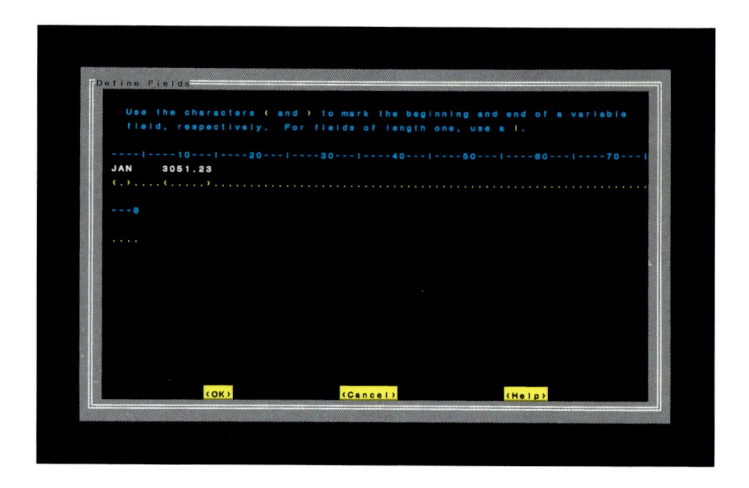

9. Define each field in the external file.

Enter a name and a label. For example, replace V1 with *Month*, and enter *Sales month* for label.

Scroll forward to define the next field. (Select **Keys** from the Help pull-down menu to find the key for scrolling.)

Enter the name, format, informat,* and label for the second field, as shown in the window above.

10. To read in the data and create the data set, select **Locals**.

When the Locals pull-down menu appears, select **Create new data set**.

---

* A format determines how the values appear; an informat determines how the values are read in.

11. In the Create new data set window, select **OK**.

    SAS/ASSIST software responds with a message indicating the number of observations read into the SAS data set. Press the ENTER key.

    Select **File** in the action bar. When the File pull-down menu appears, select **End**.

Entering Data Interactively

If your data are not already in a file, you can create a SAS data set by entering the data interactively, as follows:

1. From the Primary Menu, select **DATA MGMT**.
2. From the Data Management Menu, select **CREATE/IMPORT**.
3. From the Create/Import Menu, select **Enter data interactively**.
4. In the Enter Data Interactively window, select **Enter data in tabular form**. The following window appears:

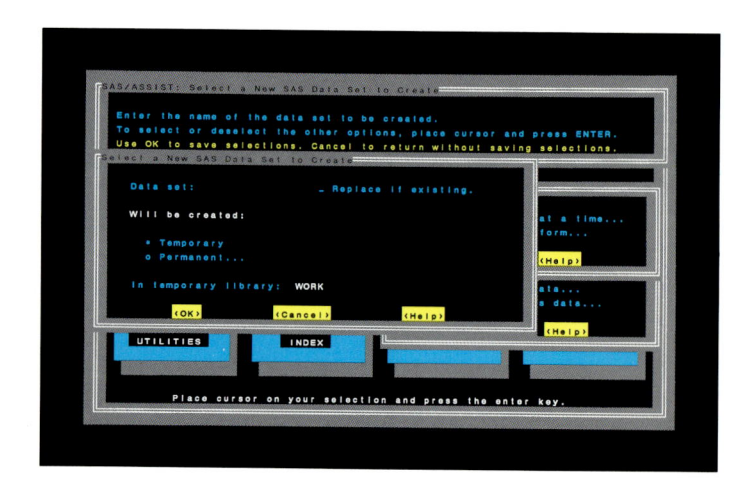

a. Enter the name of the SAS data set (for example, GSALES).
b. Select **Permanent**. The software displays a list of your available SAS data libraries. Select the data library you just created (see page 39).
c. Select **OK**.

Getting Started with SAS/ASSIST Software **45**

5. In the Define a New SAS Data Set window, define each variable as shown next.

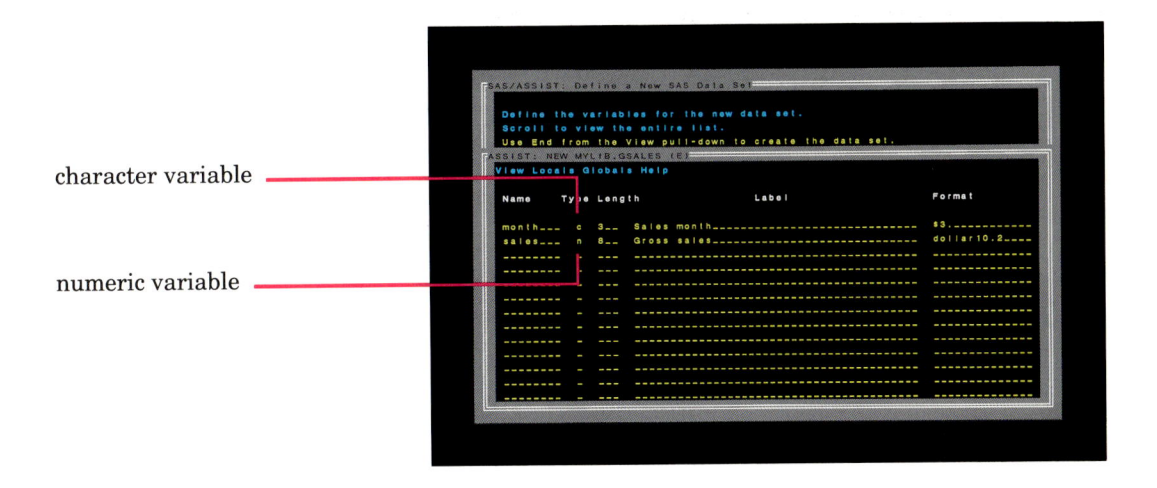

character variable —

numeric variable —

6. Select **Locals** in the action bar. When the Locals pull-down menu appears, select **Format/Informat**.*

Enter the informat for the SALES variable as shown above.

---

* A format determines how the values appear; an informat determines how the values are entered.

7. Select **View** in the action bar. When the View pull-down menu appears, select **End** to create the data set.
8. Start entering the data as shown below.

```
FSVIEW:  MYLIB.GSALES  (E)
File Edit Search View Locals Globals Help
         MONTH        SALES
          jan        $3,051.23
          feb         2813.50
```

After you type in the value (3051.23) and press ENTER, the software uses the format for the field (DOLLAR10.2) to display the dollar sign correctly.

9. When you have finished entering the data, select **File** in the action bar. When the File pull-down menu appears, select **End**.

Now that you have your data in a SAS data set, you are ready to use SAS/ASSIST software to manage, analyze, and present them.

SAS/ASSIST® Software — Your Window to Greater Productivity

It's Easy to Use
- You just point and select.
- SAS/ASSIST software prompts for the information it needs.
- Context-sensitive help is available at every step.
- There's no programming syntax to learn or remember.

It's Extendable
You can use the EIS option to develop SAS System applications quickly and to make them available to other SAS/ASSIST software users at your site.

It's a Training Tool
SAS/ASSIST software provides an online tutorial that teaches the fundamentals of the SAS System.

In addition, SAS/ASSIST software generates commented SAS language programs that can help users learn the SAS language.

It's Part of the SAS System
SAS/ASSIST software is part of the SAS System, so it brings the power of the SAS System to bear on your work.

And, as with the SAS System, if you can use SAS/ASSIST software on one operating system, you can use it on any operating system. There may be some differences in appearance, depending on your hardware and operating system, but the software itself works the same on any computer system.

The SAS System includes capabilities for

Data Access
- ☐ transparent database access
- ☐ raw data file access
- ☐ data communications.

Data Management
- ☐ data entry, retrieval, editing, and query
- ☐ data handling utilities
- ☐ data formatting and conversion.

Data Analysis
- ☐ statistics
- ☐ mathematical programming
- ☐ forecasting and modeling
- ☐ linear programming
- ☐ experimental design
- ☐ business planning
- ☐ financial management and analysis
- ☐ decision support
- ☐ project management
- ☐ operations research
- ☐ statistical quality improvement
- ☐ computer performance evaluation and capacity planning.

Data Presentation
- ☐ automated and ad hoc report writing
- ☐ business and analytical graphics
- ☐ mapping
- ☐ business correspondence.

SAS Institute backs its software with several kinds of **training** including instructor-, video-, and computer-based courses, as well as continuous free **technical support** via phone, mail, or dial-up computer access.

Also, you can obtain a wide range of **consulting services**, from statistical design and analysis to large-scale applications development.

Index

A
applications
   creating   27
   running   27

B
bar charts
   example of producing   8-13
   producing   20
BY groups   3, 32

C
calendars, creating   20
control chart, example   26

D
data analysis   23-24
DATA ANALYSIS option   23-24
data libraries
   See SAS data libraries
data management   17-18
DATA MGMT option   17-18
data sets
   See SAS data sets
database access   17

E
EIS option   27
executive information system   27
EXIT option   31
experimental design   25

F
files
   See SAS data sets
footnotes, specifying   6
forecasting   25
function keys   30

G
GANTT chart, example   25
graphics
   example of producing   8-13
   producing   21-22
   replaying   21
   types   21
graphics device, selecting   10
GRAPHICS option   8, 21-22

H
HELP option   3, 32

I
importing files   40-44
INDEX option
   individual menus   9, 32
   Primary Menu   3, 31

L
labels, creating   20
loan analysis   25

M
maps, example of producing   21-22

O
operations research   25
output
   customizing   6-7
   recalling stored   28

P
pie charts, producing   20, 21
planning tools   25-26
PLANNING TOOLS option   25-26
Primary Menu   2, 15
   option descriptions   15-32
programs, stored
   executing   28
   managing   28
   modifying   28
   recalling   28
programs, storing   4, 28
project management   25
pull-down menus, selecting from   5

R
regression analysis, example   23
REPORT WRITING option   3, 19-20
reports
   example of producing   3-5
   producing   19-20
   specifying page dimensions for   6
   specifying titles for   6-7
   types   20
RESULTS option   28-29

S
SAS data libraries   30
   creating your own   37-39
SAS data sets
   browsing   17
   combining   18
   editing   17
   entering data in   44-46
   sorting   18, 30
   with data for maps, example   17
SAS data sets, creating   17
   by importing data   40-44
   interactively   40, 44-46
SAS/ASSIST software
   as a training tool   47
   exiting   31
   invoking   35-37
   Primary Menu options   15-32
   requirements for running   33
SETUP option   30
statistics   23
subsetting data   3, 32

T
tables, example of producing   19-20
titles, specifying   6-7
TUTORIAL option   16

U
UTILITIES option   9, 32

W
WHERE processing   32